W9-AQL-768

Date: 2/13/15

NAVAJO

Big Buddy Books
An Imprint of Abdo Publishing
www.abdopublishing.com

Sarah Tieck

www.abdopublishing.com

Published by Abdo Publishing, a division of ABDO, PO Box 398166, Minneapolis, Minnesota 55439.
Copyright © 2015 by Abdo Consulting Group, Inc. International copyrights reserved in all countries. No part
of this book may be reproduced in any form without written permission from the publisher. Big Buddy Books™
is a trademark and logo of Abdo Publishing.

Printed in the United States of America, North Mankato, Minnesota.
052014
092014

THIS BOOK CONTAINS
RECYCLED MATERIALS

Cover Photo: © Chuck Place/Alamy.
Interior Photos: © Tom Bean/Alamy (p. 27); Getty Images (pp. 5, 9, 15, 16, 17, 19, 29); © NativeStock.com/Angel
    Wynn (pp. 13, 21); © nsf/Alamy (pp. 25, 30); © Sheryl Savas/Alamy (p. 26); Shutterstock (pp. 11, 23).

Coordinating Series Editor: Rochelle Baltzer
Contributing Editors: Bridget O'Brien, Marcia Zappa
Graphic Design: Adam Craven

Library of Congress Cataloging-in-Publication Data

Tieck, Sarah, 1976
  Navajo / Sarah Tieck.
      pages cm.
   ISBN 978-1-62403-355-1
1. Navajo Indians--Juvenile literature. I. Title.
   E99.N3T54 2014
   979.1004'9726--dc23
                          2014005026

CONTENTS

Amazing People

Hundreds of years ago, North America was mostly wild, open land. Native Americans lived on the land. They had their own languages and **customs**.

The Navajo (NA-vuh-hoh) are a Native American nation. They are known for their beautiful art and strong leaders. Let's learn more about these Native Americans.

Did You Know?

The Navajo call themselves *Diné*. This means "the people."

Navajo women are known for their beautiful craftwork. They have been making baskets and rugs for hundreds of years.

Navajo Territory

At first, the Navajo lived in Canada. Between 1100 and 1500, they moved south. They made their homelands in the southwestern United States.

The people lived in an area known as the Four Corners. This is where present-day New Mexico, Arizona, Colorado, and Utah meet. Land in the Southwest has mountains, deserts, canyons, and forests. It is rich in **minerals**.

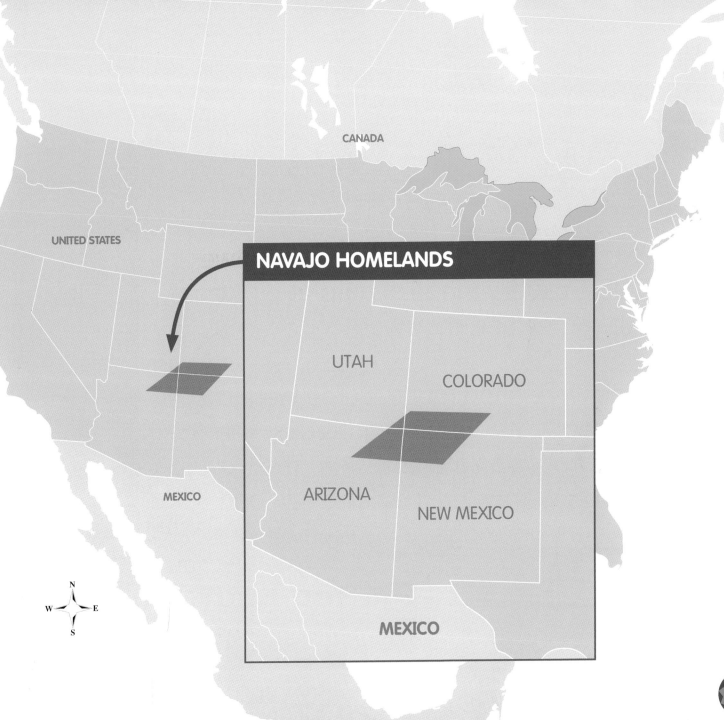

CANADA

UNITED STATES

NAVAJO HOMELANDS

UTAH

COLORADO

ARIZONA

NEW MEXICO

MEXICO

MEXICO

N
W • E
S

7

HOME LIFE

The Navajo lived in homes called hogans. These were usually made of mud or dirt and logs. But sometimes, they were made of stones.

Hogans were often round. Some were a rounded shape with six or eight sides. The door was always on the east side. The Navajo believed this welcomed the rising sun and brought them blessings.

Did You Know?

Some hogans were built specially for ceremonies.

Most hogans measured about 20 feet (6 m) in diameter.

What They Ate

The Navajo were mainly farmers. Their crops included corn, beans, and squash. They also grew fruit, such as peaches.

In addition, men hunted deer, prairie dogs, rabbits, and mountain goats. The women gathered berries and other wild plants.

Did You Know?

Early Navajo were not farmers. When they moved to the Southwest, they learned farming from the Pueblo people.

Have you ever tried gardening? The Navajo did all their planting and tending by hand.

Corn is also known as maize.

11

The Navajo farmed mostly during the summer. The fields flooded with water, which helped the crops grow. The people also raised animals such as sheep and goats. These provided wool, meat, and milk.

Can you imagine making yarn? The Navajo spun sheep's wool into yarn. Then, they used the yarn to make clothing, rugs, and blankets.

13

DAILY LIFE

The Navajo had different jobs. Some were farmers, warriors, hunters, leaders, or **medicine men**. Others learned to make art, such as silver jewelry. Navajo women were especially known for their weaving skills.

Learning was important for Navajo children. They learned by watching the adults and elders. They helped with chores. Children also played games and had dolls and toys.

The Navajo often wore colorful woven clothing. They also wore woven blankets and sashes.

MADE BY HAND

The Navajo made the objects they needed for daily life. They are especially known for their creativity and artistry.

Silver Jewelry

The Navajo are skilled silversmiths. They learned to make silver jewelry from the Spanish. They often combine silver with turquoise to make beautiful, one-of-a-kind jewelry.

Woven Baskets

Navajo basketmakers weave plant materials into beautiful designs. Some baskets are used to hold things. Others are used for special ceremonies, such as weddings.

Colorful Rugs

The Navajo wove beautiful rugs. They learned this skill from other Native American tribes, such as the Pueblo. Navajo women are among the best weavers in the world.

Painted Pottery

The Navajo are famous for the painted patterns on their pottery. The pots sometimes have special meaning. They can be used for holding water and other purposes.

Spirit Life

Religion was important to the Navajo way of life. The people prayed, sang, danced, and made art to honor their gods.

The tribe's **medicine men** led dances, **rituals**, and **ceremonies**. Sometimes a ceremony included one or two people. Other times, it included thousands of Navajo. A ceremony was meant to heal people and bring them blessings.

Today, the Navajo make colorful sand paintings for some ceremonies. The sacred paintings are destroyed after the ceremony. The Navajo believe this returns the painting's powers to the earth.

19

Storytellers

   The Navajo told stories. These stories could teach people history or lessons. Some simply entertained them. Sometimes, stories were shared through pottery designs or other art. For many years, they weren't written down.

   The Navajo are known for their stories about evil beings called skinwalkers. They believe skinwalkers wear animal skins and travel at night. Some Navajo believe it is bad luck to speak of them.

Today, elders are expected to share stories with younger Navajo.

FIGHTING FOR LAND

Spanish settlers first met the Navajo in the 1600s. The Navajo did not like their **customs**, and sometimes the Spanish took them as **slaves**. Together with the Pueblo and Apache tribes, they fought off Spanish settlers.

In the 1800s, American soldiers and settlers began to move west. They traveled through and settled on Navajo land. The Navajo were strong fighters. They often attacked them to **protect** their land and way of life. The US government wanted to stop these attacks.

The Navajo attacked Spanish settlements along the
Rio Grande river. They took their horses and livestock.

In 1864, the US government forced the Navajo off their land. They made them walk more than 300 miles (480 km) to a small, poor **reservation** in New Mexico. This sad event is now called the Long Walk. About 2,000 Navajo died on the walk and at the reservation.

The Navajo fought to get their homeland back. Chief Manuelito worked with the US government. Today, the Navajo have the largest reservation in the United States. They have more than 24,000 square miles (62,000 sq km) of land in New Mexico, Arizona, and Utah.

 Chief Manuelito believed in education for his people. He worked with the US government so the Navajo could return to their homeland.

25

BACK IN TIME

1861

Navajo leaders, including Chief Manuelito, signed papers saying they would stop fighting with the US Army.

1923

The Navajo established a tribal government. It was considered one of the most advanced Native American governments.

1864

US soldiers forced 8,000 Native Americans off their land. The Navajo walked more than 300 miles (480 km). In 2005, the Bosque Redondo Memorial (*left*) opened in New Mexico to help people remember the Long Walk.

1968

Diné College opened in Arizona. It is the first community college owned and run by Native Americans.

1967

The National Park Service bought the Hubbell Trading Post National Historic Site. The trading post had opened in 1878 on the Navajo **reservation**. Today, it is the longest continuously operating trading post.

2010

The US government counted about 287,000 Navajo living in the country.

A Strong Nation

The Navajo people have a long, rich history. They are known for their woven rugs and silver jewelry. They are a large, strong nation.

Navajo roots run deep. Today, the people have kept alive those special things that make them Navajo. Even though times have changed, many people carry the **traditions**, stories, and memories of the past into the present.

Navajo women often use baskets in traditional dances.

"My children, education is the ladder to all our needs. Tell our people to take it."

— Chief Manuelito

Glossary

ceremony a formal event on a special occasion.

custom a practice that has been around a long time and is common to a group or a place.

medicine man a Native American healer and spiritual leader.

mineral a natural substance that makes up rocks and other parts of nature.

protect (pruh-TEHKT) to guard against harm or danger.

reservation (reh-zuhr-VAY-shuhn) a piece of land set aside by the government for Native Americans to live on.

ritual (RIH-chuh-wuhl) a formal act or set of acts that is repeated.

slave a person who is bought and sold as property.

tradition (truh-DIH-shuhn) a belief, a custom, or a story handed down from older people to younger people.

Websites

To learn more about Native Americans, visit **booklinks.abdopublishing.com**. These links are routinely monitored and updated to provide the most current information available.

31

INDEX